Banquet of Mercy for the Universe

This volume contains selected poems from the following collections of Hanane Aad's poetry, originally written in Arabic:

My Freedom I Carry in My Mouth, Dergham Editions, Beirut, Lebanon, 2010

Pearls of the Soul Riding Virtue, Al-Ibdaa Editions, Beirut, Lebanon, 2005

Like a Grain of Wheat, Kleudge Editions, Beirut, Lebanon, 1998

Hanane Aad

Banquet of Mercy for the Universe

Banquet of Mercy for the Universe

© 2022 Hanane Aad

English translation © 2015 Peter Waugh and Hanane Aad

Texianer Verlag

Tuningen, Germany

www.texianer.com

ISBN: 978-3-949197-98-7

All rights reserved. This book or parts thereof, may not be reproduced for commercial purposes in any form or by any means, electronic or mechanical, including photocopying, recording, or any information storage or retrieval system now known or to be invented, without written permission from the publisher

For

my father and my mother

Contents

"Lay Down Your Arms"! 11

Part 1

The Mill of the Soul 19

Part 2

Wish 29
Hymn for a Love 31
Purple Compassion 37
A Rainbow in Your Veins 41
Nature's Tenderness 45

Part 3

The Orbits of the Soul 49
Who Will Buy Me Certainty? 51
Self-Sacrifice 53
Madness 55
The Dance of Destiny 57
Refuge 59

Part 4

Elevation 63
The Violin of Absence 65
Banquet of Mercy for the Universe 67

Part 5

Hallucination 71

The Feral Darkness	73
The Tools of Patience	75
The Pulse of Eternity	77
A Scarf for the Soul	79
Tent of the Light	81

Part 6

Love's Spark	85
The Child of Time	87

Part 7

A Pearl from her Hand	91
The Poets' Mercy	93

Appendix

About Hanane Aad	95
About Hanane Aad's Poetry	99

"Lay Down Your Arms"!

POETRY. PEACE. Poetry starts with the letter P. Peace starts with the same letter. Poetry might be the language of the soul. Peace might be the soul of the universe. Is it simply a coincidence that the two words both start with the same letter, with P? I think not. Then P is the common starting letter for POETRY and PEACE. However, the word power also starts with the letter P. POETRY, PEACE, POWER. Poetry might be the power of peace. Peace might be the power of poetry. The power of poetry might bring peace. The power of peace might bring poetry. Poetry might empower peace. How can poetry empower peace? How can poetry spread reconciliation through peace, or peace through reconciliation? Reconciliation between human beings? Peace between civilisations? Reconciliation between cultures? Reconciliation and peace between citizens in the same country or nation?

If one agrees that poetry is in general a very meaningful and powerful and appreciated part of almost all cultures, civilisations and societies, this means that poetry must have a role to play in the history of humanity and the history of the nations, as well as in the itinerary of individuals. Even the politicians and the decision-makers in all states and societies, or at least many of them, often show great appreciation for poetry and poets. Not only that, but many of these personalities also frequently use excerpts from ancient or modern poetry to endorse their ideas, opinions or points of view. Therefore, it might be said that poetry is one of the most influential arts in a variety of cultures and societies.

Guns and bombs are the weapons of wars. POETRY is a weapon of PEACE. Poetry always remains the inner human voice which opens doors for life and rejects all forms of war and destruction. Poetry was, is, and always will be a wonderful vehicle for the values and magical beauty which are able to evolve inside men and women that will of life, will of love, will of peace, against all that denies the values of both life and love. It is the will of life and love which is able to bring peace and reconciliation. Poetry and war are certainly two strong opposites, except when poetry is also a way to fight against all kinds of injustice and oppression and dictatorship. Someone who grew up in a culture which appreciates and respects poetry will not be someone who easily becomes involved in any kind of war or absurd conflict or violent acts. Such a person will not easily agree to carry weapons and kill and destroy.

When talking about the bond between Literature and Peace, and especially between Poetry and Peace, one of the first images which immediately comes to my mind is that of Alfred Nobel, the founder of the Nobel Prizes. This ingenious scientist who invented an explosive which he named 'dynamite' and which brought him a huge fortune and fame, was the same man who wrote poetry and drama and had a passion for literature, but his father was not pleased with Alfred's interest in poetry, and wanted him to become a chemical engineer. Nobel, who spent all his life working on scientific experiments and registered 355 patents, ended up writing in his will that "much of his fortune was to be used to give prizes to those who have done their best for humanity" in different fields, including literature and peace. He established a prize to be dedicated to "the person who shall have done the most or the best work for fraternity between nations, for the abolition or reduction of standing armies and for the holding and promotion of peace congresses".

When reading about how Alfred Nobel also dedicated prizes to peace and literature, one is struck by two facts in his biography that might have been the strongest turning points in his life, and constituted the spark which led him to dedicate part of his fortune to peace makers and peace promoters, and another part to a great body of work in literature which has often been awarded for great work in poetry.

The first fact is that some of his experiments caused accidents that killed several people, including his younger brother. The second is the lifelong friendship that Alfred Nobel established with his one-time secretary, the Austrian Bertha von Suttner, with whom he later exchanged letters for many years. She became involved and very active in the peace movement, and wrote the famous book *Lay Down Your Arms*.

On the one hand, there is dynamite which is a massively dangerous and destructive weapon in war. On the other hand, there are the awards for those who have done their best for humanity and for fraternity between nations. A contradictory picture but also one of the deepest messages, and a strong lesson to learn, behind which stands the potential poet Alfred Nobel!

We move from the expression above "massively dangerous and destructive weapon", to its opposite "massively peaceful and constructive weapon", in order to look at the role which poetry activities and festivals play in building bridges to peace. In that respect, the International Poetry Festival of Medellin seems to be a very meaningful and powerful proof that poetry is really able to bring about peace and reconciliation. The crowds of people we see every year as a huge audience during the festival readings and activities tell us indirectly about people's aspiration for peace and serenity as expressed through their love for poetry. One can read on their enchanted faces and in their delighted eyes that kind of charming thirst for serenity, for peace, for the *joie de vivre*. I myself come from a land, Lebanon, which suffered decades of war, which witnessed destruction, cruelty, great loss of life and all the kinds of pain that human beings bear – cannot bear! – in war. May Colombia soon win the battle for a sustainable peace empowered also by its poets and the International Poetry Festival of Medellin which has always led a very noble fight for peace, employing poetry as its only weapon.

I believe it is worth trying, through poetry, to tame violence and hate, to convert them into a pure will of the generations to build a future on the authentic basis of prosperity and serenity, on the sacred respect for the life of all human beings everywhere and at all times. I believe that we can all start to give our children little poetry books as gifts instead of presents which are directly or indirectly symbols of war and violent conflict. I believe that we should tell our children that even toy weapons, virtual and electronic war games, or even just violent games, are in a way harmful to the global spirit of beauty in our universe.

Why not all cry, with Bertha von Suttner: "Lay Down Your Arms"!

Let this be, for us as poets and through poetry, that powerful cry in the universe that

*"will make the guns fall blind and deaf,
maybe even death, racing towards a baby, will
protest its action and disown itself, noticing on
the little one's face a smile that makes it
crumble"*.[1]

HANANE AAD
Lebanon/Austria
© November 2016

NOTE This article was originally written for the magazine of the International Poetry Festival of Medellin, Colombia, in which Hanane Aad took part in 2017.

---

1   Excerpt from Hanane Aad's poem entitled "Hymn for a Love" from her book *Pearls of the Soul Riding Virtue*, published in 2005. Translation by Peter Waugh and Hanane Aad.

Why did I forget, or am I about to forget, that I am now,

or from now on, a warm and free hand,

whose pen will raise it to the apogee of joy and freedom!

Part 1

The Mill of the Soul

Now "I am dead I notice" that I have started to be able to dedicate myself to the writing, since this moment, the moment I moved to the river banks, of which I was always dreaming, and had wasted a whole life before reaching.

O God! How comfortable I feel because I died, because I finally took down from my shoulders the charge of what is called life, or world... Could you believe that a great happiness covered me in my coffin? Could you believe that in my deep death I found my pen pushed miraculously into my cold closed hand?

Am I to believe that only my right hand regained its warmth? I don't know how it differs from my body's warmth when I was still alive... O God! Am I to believe, or would you believe with me, that death transformed me into a warm hand just when I understood at the moment of crossing that I am now able to write till drunkenness, till ecstasy, till ardour, till freedom, till crying, till madness, till childhood, till divinity, or rather till all these together!

Please, let me believe that only my pen, which is

not a part of my entity, accompanied me to my cemetery, that I am the warm hand which carried its pen till death, that I am the free hand whose faithful pen broke through the high and impenetrable border between life and death. Let me believe that my beautiful and friendly pen, my pen so tender, so honest, so generous, so full of unbelievable sincerity ever since my early youth, that it came here with me.

O! It is my right hand to which the warmth came back after my death, a warmth not like my body's warmth when it was still alive! Now I remember that I always wore my watch on my right hand! How lucky I am! My hand's warmth and my pen and the watch that I always wore in my right hand! Just now I understood why! So that I would have the time here! The whole time! In my right hand I have carried the time till here!

But why do I feel dizzy with happiness?! Even though I have no head now. I am rather a warm hand which will write with its warmth and its pen all that the woman to whom it belongs could not write when she was still in the heart of life. O! My watch was always on my right hand, so that I could hold the time whenever I liked. I wanted to master time and turn its two hands myself, the small one and the big one as well, just as a true poetess turns the mill of the soul.

Why did I forget, or am I about to forget, that I am now, or from now on, a warm and free hand, whose pen will raise it to the apogee of joy and freedom! Why not, since the pen fulfilled the prophecy of accompanying the one we love until death! That is right, I paid no attention to asking whether it was the pen itself that loved me until death, or me who loved the pen until death? But, why all these questions?! What is important is that somebody loved somebody else until death, and even after death, so at least the saying, or the prophecy – I don't know exactly which – won't become a dead tradition! Yes, the crucial thing is that I now have the freedom of writing, and also have white time rising from the watch which I always wore on my right hand without knowing for a long time why.

God! In the name of your God... I ask you forgiveness! I forgot for a moment that you are the God of gods, but tell me please, should I write by my hea...rt (*qal...bi*)? Or by my pen (*qalami*)? Just now I understood! Rather, at this moment I realized that I must have died, in order to notice that there is only a small difference between my pen and my heart! Only one letter!!! And what must I know more? It would be enough that the letter M (Arabic *Mim*) slips from my pen, and then opens and becomes a B (Arabic *Ba*) till I start to write from my heart! How beautiful it is to write from my heart! How dangerous it is too!

But I won't care! From it I will write that the babies and the birds and the mothers and the angels were all created from the same clay, and I won't forget the gazelles either, nor the flowers or the butterflies. Oh! I forgot that the voice of Feyrouz was also (and especially) created from the same clay. By the way, to mention her pleasant and dulcet voice even though I am dead, means that her voice is here with me too!

I see myself feeling my smile in the warmth of my hand! I smile because I always repeated in front of my close friends when I was still alive, that if the voice of Feyrouz won't be in paradise, then paradise will loose its radiance in my eyes, and I won't feel happy at all in paradise without that voice! But how naïve I am! How do I think I would go to paradise? Rather how far away is the idea that paradise exists!

And I don't know why, at this instant, I enjoy singing this excerpt from a song, *The Bird of Paradise:*

> *Freedom, you flower of fire*
> *You savage baby*
> *Freedom, we went out to see the sun*
> *We went out to meet the wind…*

Also singing "Forget? How can I forget that for fifteen years I was alive and not alive, for fifteen years life went on, summers and winters, but without me… And it was so cold that I was not able to sleep at nights, I was painting a big sun on the walls, in order to sit close to it and get warm!

I remember now that I wrote when I was still alive that "The hymn has the aroma of freedom, I long to smell my freedom before my final sleep." I also realized that it was me who "was alive and not alive, and summers and winters were coming and leaving without me..." It is true that the wonderful lady sang this on my behalf. And the proof is that the memory of the cold still bites me cynically till now even though I have no body!

I remember that, ever since I was a little girl, I always liked to associate the adjective cynical with the cold. To this day, I still insist only on this adjective when speaking about the cold! It is the most cynical one, and the most savage too! Is it meaningless that mothers get up from their enjoyable sleep at night in order to put the warm cover back on the bodies of their children?

To return to the creatures that are all created from the same clay. There is a very important common factor which brings them all together: their wings and their flying! I would like to start with the mothers. Their tenderness grows wings for them so that they fly through the universe, and flap their wings offering clemency, and devote themselves wholeheartedly to taking care of its survival!

"... and I adore my life because if I were to die I would be ashamed before my mother's tears"! Oh God how will I be able to cry now? All the tears of the universe are nothing compared to all that splendour sparkling from these words. Because if I died I would be ashamed before my mother's tears! Even here I am still shedding rivers of tears, but in return, I cannot give this amazing, vast and poetic waterfall even a little bit of its great tenderness!

Let me hallucinate that perhaps Mahmoud Darwish surpassed all of them with this poetic lightning, and perhaps I would have seen him, the same Mahmoud Darwish, if this were all that he wrote! Yes, and a thousand times yes! It is enough that one invents this expression to become a poet. No! no! The point is not in creation or in utterance – it is not only in utterance! Rather, it is in the miracle of exhuming the fact of being ashamed before one's mother's tears.

As if I see him dying for an instant and experiencing the feeling of that shame. Because if I were to die I would feel ashamed in front of my mother's tears. Oh God, did you not feel your heart gleeful before all this tenderness streaming from this image?

So my whole entity is now metamorphosed into a living hand, extremely happy to enjoy the time coming generously from my watch. Why am I imagining myself flying very high, on the wing of the rainbow, glittering even in no sky!

Why am I amusing myself by flying, and with the

rainbow's light instead of writing? Did I not dream all my life of enjoying even a narrow space of tranquility where I would go to join my abundant poems crowded in my head and my heart and my conscience? I can see them clearly right now, one by one, getting ready to throw themselves onto my white pages.

Yet how come I was always able to perceive, while still alive, that my poem, even if it calls me for a long time to give it a body, will never depart, but rather will be patient with me, and is extremely kind to be so patient, as if my poems were not temporal, as if our relationship were fated and obligatory, in joy as in sorrow.

How sorry I am for my abundant poems, which waited for me a whole life long and were so patient with me! Nonetheless, it is good that I am now able to meet them, to take them in my arms, to listen to them, to apologize to them. But I will also tell them that they were always inside me, while I was living, that I always felt their breath in my chest, that I eyed their lights and shadows, their joys and sadness through the little tears of the soul! It is also good that I died, so that I don't lose them, so that I would have the time to write them down.

What a luxury! One that I could not have during my life! Or rather, it was not luxury that I wanted, I just wished to have a few breaks, even only a few, to free myself from the absurd circle of the crowd and the labyrinth, and have the time to take my poem's hand, and give it my hand, so that there would thus be the certainty of pulse and existence.

Is poetry a path toward the certainty of my existence? I hope it will be, even partly, or perhaps it is the only thing that makes me realize that I once lived. It is full of my itinerary, of my steps, full of my breath, following a gleam, following a smile, following a moon which is vowed only to me.

Even here, in the quietness of death, I see myself living fully in my poems' leaven, in the redolent smoke of an incense I myself created during my many fearful exiles, in my intense isolations.

So now I am a right hand, and a watch, the heart of which is white, and a pen without an equal in its honesty, and a caravan of poems which came into me before breaking through the darkness of this universe and never cared for anything, except the rhythms of my soul and the rhythms of my own hymns....

Part 2

Love me, my love,

and the greatest virtue

will reach its true sphere

Wish

The earth smells of slumber,

the hymn has the aroma of freedom.

I long to smell my freedom

before my final sleep.

I long to sing my hymn

before the earth covers me.

Hymn for a Love

To love
is to be forever
gripped in the fist of yearning,
to burn in the flames of desire,
to be hurled
into impossible distance
at the insistence of memory,
to be drowned forever
in a fidelity
expansive as the sea,
to weep to the last tears
and fear not their unending.

Love me, my love,
the stars will rise
on their way to the wedding,
children fall asleep on serenity's shoulder.
Love me, my love
and those loves

that lie waiting on the heart's threshold
will awaken.

Love me, my love,

the earth of the poor will yield up gold

to serve them as a sword

in the face of deprivation

and vanquish the sword of oppression.

Love me, my love,

murderers will be consumed

in the fire of their hate,

hurl themselves into the river of regret

and cure themselves of that other leprosy.

Love me, my love,

and mourning mothers will embrace,

even if only in a fleeting dream,

the faces of disappeared loved-ones.

Perhaps the chests of slaves dying in misery

will be liberated on the rock of subjection.

Love me, my love,

and the birds of the earth

will escape the cruelty of their hunters,

their twitter, so innocent and tender,

will make the guns fall blind and deaf,

maybe even death, racing towards a baby,

will protest its action and disown itself,

noticing on the little one's face

a smile that makes it crumble.

Love me, my love,

water my eyes

with the clearest tenderness,

tighten my forehead with a kiss

that miraculously transforms

into a splendid crown on my head.

Love me, my love,

and the universe will find repose

in the arms of divinity,

cured, at least for one moment,

of the tumours of cruelty

in its mortal body.

Love me, my love,

and the greatest virtue

will reach its true sphere.

Love me, my love,

and the universe will rise in protest

at its agonies,

tear off its terrifying masks,

cast its illusions

back into the jaws of the fire,

and impose on history

the alphabet of salvation.

Purple Compassion

My eyes a den of amazement,

my smile the honesty of the sceptre,

I myself a violin suspended

between the quivering soul

and the pulse of strings.

Raise me upon your palms

with all the force of a last wager,

paint childhood's fertile pastures

with your purple tenderness,

fill the moment's pitchers

with eternally flowing wine.

Give my lips a mythical cut,

invent for my face

a horizon white as virtue,

carry me in your breast

like a delicious secret,

and take refuge in its shadow

whenever you lack tenderness,

let me vanish and hide

between your bones,

like spring ascending your veins,

take me each dawn

to your serenity,

savour the rain of my memory,

let its warmth bestow comfort

on the cold soul.

Bear me to the summit of your hopes,

use the rays of my eyelashes

to conquer the emperors of cruelty,

with the clearness of my heart

purge this universe lacerated by mist,

wait for me there

in the evenings of other times

where new lives are bejewelled,

wait for me there,

on the edge of the absolute,

hold me there in my entirety,

sing and dance with me,

celebrating an encounter

encompassed by the eternal,

by the union of freedom and certainty.

A Rainbow in Your Veins

I vanish behind my childhood,

my heart rises high as my lips,

each time I smile to you

it dances within my eyes.

It is more than a smile,

more distant than a glance,

more profound…

I attach myself

to the shadows of a smile,

so as not to face cruelty.

Smile to me,

so that angels may come to rest

at the door of my heart.

Stride ahead, my man

and in the evening

return home to me.

Walk, bearing my eyes

on the palm of eternity.

Protect within your heart

a tomorrow, gamboling towards us

like a gazelle at play.

Stride ahead, stride ahead,

do not fear the storm.

Free yourself of their jealousy,

it is like dust, nothing more.

Stride ahead, my man,

whose heart is so handsome,

listen well to the sound of time

caressing my forehead.

It will always draw me

as a rainbow in your veins,

a rainbow you follow

in amazement and shadow,

and secretly always travel

to the enchantress of light.

Nature's Tenderness

After some moments

we have to leave the place.

The tree looks at us.

We both go

with dew on our hair.

The leaves weep,

saying farewell.

Part 3

Spray me like rays of love

where coldness, darkness and

flagellation prevail.

The Orbits of the Soul

My true star circles

in the orbits of the soul.

That is where I wander at dawn,

there I park my tired caravan.

My mysterious and faithful star

awaits me always

at the turnings of time,

on the slopes of the storm.

My true star

circles in the orbits of the soul,

in its presence I kneel,

I murmur,

and read the canticle of quintessence,

I plunge into the ocean of being

the soul of supreme tenderness,

I embrace the illusions of freedom,

wash them with my soft tears

till they gleam pure.

May they save me,

may they raise me

to the arc lights of certainty.

Who Will Buy Me Certainty?

I am the eternally anxious one –

who will buy me certainty?

Where can I obtain the serenity of silence?

Who will build me kingdoms of quiet?

How can I gain victory over the labyrinth?

I am the eternally anxious one,

calling myself every morning

from the slumber of the continents,

from the ultimate shores

to the ocean's pulse.

My pulse is the pulse of anxiety,

so how can I mould for my eyelids

the soundness of sleep?

Within me is the anxiety of eternity,

so how can I transport myself

to fields of jasmine and tulips?

I am the eternally anxious one –

who will lend me the elixir of patience?

How can I arrive at the port of ports?

Can I succeed in climbing

into the depths of smiling grace?

I am the eternally anxious one –

when will I banish

the darkness of entity?

When will I carry my soul

to the paradise of the soul?

When will eternity play for me

the melody of melodies,

to the eternity of eternity?

Self-Sacrifice

My face broke long ago.

For ages I lived without my face,

could not cry,

because my eyes were broken too.

Mirrors grew dumb

and locked their worlds away.

My face shattered,

the universe quaked,

my face shattered

and my heart heard

the steps of the frost approaching

but refused to resist.

It said: break me, as you did the face,

but spray me like rays of love

where coldness,

darkness and flagellation prevail.

Plant my remains in the desert

and the miracle will come to pass

and the sand will bear

lilies and jasmine.

Sprinkle my blood

around the edges of the wound

and through my wounds

I will become balsam.

Madness

The hand of the clock

is a second Nero.

It orders the kingdom

to be burnt.

The legions are defeated,

stumble over tears

on their way back.

The dragon Time

tears innocence apart

and assassinates the blue.

Time attacks

the pure forehead,

stealing its brilliance.

The egoist deems

great God his own,

the others —

all the others —

are blasphemous,

crazy.

He orders their execution.

The Dance of Destiny

I threw my memory to the planet

and its cry crept back

to my ears as silence

resounding till it pained me.

My memory,

the self who committed suicide by light,

my memory,

my life, racing away fleet of foot.

My memory,

I will remember you,

pray for you,

recreate your image,

and hang it above my eyelashes,

face to face with destiny

waltzing over my eyelids.

Refuge

I surrender to the temple's silence

when my sadness moans

and all paths are smothered

by my steps' confusion.

I seek shelter in an infant's smile

each time the adults drag me

into their gloomy maturity

and O-so-pitiful philosophy.

I take refuge in an ancient icon

when day disowns its dawn

and night rejects its saints.

I catch at a bird's warbling

when the storm thrusts me

towards anger's madness.

I catch at a mother's prayers

each time the war throws me

to cruelty's volcano.

I cling to the beauty of a little wing.

each time the prisons and ramparts

arise before me.

I cling to the pulse of my own veins

when the faces depart

for the mirror of nothingness.

Part 4

Strike up melodious song

for those whose hearts are blind.

Elevation

I am skilled in the art

of speaking to the dead,

of listening to them.

I see myself crossing

the borders of death,

meeting them,

touching their disappointment,

dancing with their white joy,

questioning their tears.

They respond:

"We the dead

don't die,

we disappear behind the silence.

We don't leave,

we see

we hear

we feel.

We suffer because of the wound.

We only die when we are forgotten.

We lament the absence of the living,

but we don't betray

the wall of silence,

for only there

lies the nobility of death."

The Violin of Absence

After my death

I want to become a violin.

So that my soul may climb

to the verdure of its tender melody.

Perhaps I was a violin

before my birth,

or perhaps a canary,

a canary that invented its freedom

from its modesty,

or perhaps I was a piece of music

dancing in the light of its strings,

or the sound of twittering

asleep in a songbird's throat.

Perhaps, after my departure,

I will metamorphose into a smile

on the gorgeous face of an infant,

or perhaps into a breath of relief

glancing the breast of the unhappy,

or a shudder of consolation

touching the hearts of passers-by.

Banquet of Mercy for the Universe

Tomorrow I'll gather up my heart and flee,

from now on, pain will trouble its beating no more.

Cover me gently with earth, very gently,

but please keep the shovel away from my heart!

After my departure, there'll be nothing to fear,

except that my heart might get wounded.

Today I am going away,

not a care in the world for my body.

It is in my heart that I carry

all those that I love,

all those that have loved me.

So please have mercy, yet only on my heart,

in it, my last treasures,

in it, the yeast of my eclipsed life,

in it, all my moons so peaceful and sweet,

in it, the fortune of precious love.

I am the one between whose bones nests clemency,

and the challenge of finesse resides,

I am the one whose tears race the brook.

When you cover me with earth,

please return sceptre and crown to the Kingdom,

prepare a banquet of mercy for the universe,

and strike up melodious song

for those whose hearts are blind.

Part 5

Why do I add my tears

to their tears,

almost lend them my heart....?

Hallucination

My absolutism

makes me sick,

throws me

into a voracious hallucination.

Why do I involve myself

in others' pains?

Why do I think

I am them?

Why do I add my tears

to theirs,

almost reincarnate their sadness,

almost lend them my heart…?

The Feral Darkness

That man used to turn off the light

every time he saw it on.

He was either an offender or stupid.

He never realized

that his hand was extending

to my heart

and casting it into a feral darkness.

He spent his life turning off the light,

I lost my life

seeing the dark corridor

as a cave

where monsters were threatening

my bedroom every night.

He passed his life turning off the light,

I passed my life becoming sad,

suffocating, imagining the cemetery

creeping towards my home.

The Tools of Patience

I place a necklace of poetry

around the neck of the moment

and flee the limitations of time.

Aboard the enigmatic horizon

I clothe the mind with light,

I cast the lava of suspicion

into the flaming furnace.

With the tools of patience

I tame the arid deserts,

with the philosophy of generosity

I attain laurels of riches.

And at the peak of death's nihilism

I embrace the miracle of survival.

The Pulse of Eternity

Along the quay of brief time

I ride the pulse of eternity,

from the fragility of the moment

I invent motives for immortality.

Through the crack

of a gleam

I hurtle towards

the festival of light.

By the fire of my smile

I melt the direst of pains,

mould the pearls of the soul,

and spin the moment

on the loom of amazement.

A Scarf for the Soul

I have a passion for scarves,

for softness dancing in pleats.

I have a passion for scarves,

adore them like an enigma.

With love I offer them my neck,

accept to wear their neckband.

My scarf flying on my chest

is something from my soul,

floating on the forehead

of the universe.

Tent of the Light

Crossing streets crowned by lights,

my eyes shine with the Kingdom's promise,

I glimpse God's shadow flowing towards me,

feel his tenderness between my ribs,

embrace the air round his transfigured face.

The miniature lights hang generously,

seem to me like his warm and loving whisper.

I walk under the tent of the light

and imagine myself revelling in bliss.

Part 6

We and time await

our drunkenness together.

Love's Spark

The trees and the birds

have long safeguarded

a spark known as Love,

and the ducks on the lake,

floating in the night of time,

never cease teaching humans

how to dance with their age,

and also

how to float on the surface

of their melancholy.

The Child of Time

Time never tires of listening,

always waiting to get its fill of us,

so that it, too, can be.

Time always calls me:

'My little child!'

and tells me it's nothing but a void

without my magic dance

at the gates of the moment.

It murmurs in my ear that its blood

is cooled in my veins.

I am the child of time, I say:

Time tastes of the most delicious wine,

we drink it, and it drinks us,

we and time await

our drunkenness together,

till the angel of indulgence,

wholly unembarrassed,

crosses our melancholy foreheads.

Part 7

My mother is the poets' mercy.

A Pearl from her Hand

…. and so I return to my pencil,

it exchanges smiles with my fingers!

My mother follows, hurrying toward me,

carrying my ring on the palm of her hand.

Once more I fit it over my ring finger,

right at the centre sparkles a pearl

that has dropped from my mother's heart

as she was bringing it back to me again.

The Poets' Mercy

I am one whose mother

is the poetess of mercy.

My mother is the poets' mercy,

she triumphed over them

a million times.

She called me: 'My light'!

The tender woman's bones

even grew weak

from calling me every morning:

My child, my bones!

My mother whispers afar,

speaking kindly to the moon,

because she believes

the same moon sees me.

Appendix

About Hanane Aad

Hanane Aad is a Lebanese poet, journalist (Print media, radio and TV), literary critic and translator. She has lived in Vienna, Austria, since 2009. She has published 7 books: *Who Will Buy Me Certainty?* (English), April 2015 (Mumbai, India); *Duet of Flowers* (Japanese and English, 2016; in addition to 5 books published in Arabic in Beirut, Lebanon: *I Carry my Freedom in my Mouth*, 2010; *Pearls of the Soul Riding Virtue*, 2005; *Like a Grain of Wheat*, 1998; *The Echo of Nostalgia*, 1992; *Dialogue of Cultures and Love of the Language*, 2001.

She won the *Award for Excellence in Poetry at Tudor Arghezi Literature Festival 2014* in Targu Jiu in Gorj, Romania, and she received the *Award for Excellence in Foreign Poetry at the Poesis Festival of Satu Mare*, Romania, in 2011. She reads her poetry almost regularly in international poetry events and festivals in Europe, Asia and Latin America. Among the worldwide festivals she took part in: Struga Poetry Nights, Macedonia, 2010; Printemps des Poètes, Bucharest 2011; Palabra en El Mondo, Venice, 2012 and 2013; Granada International Poetry Festival, Nicaragua, 2015; Luna De Locos International Poetry Festival, Pereira,

Colombia, 2015, International Poetry Festival of Medellin, Colombia, 2017. A part of her poetry has been published in many anthologies and magazines in different countries and languages, including German, English, French, Spanish, Dutch, Italian, Russian, Japanese, Estonian, Turkish, Hindi, Bosnian, Bulgarian and Portuguese.

At the Lebanese daily newspaper An-Nahar, where she worked between 1995 and 2005, as a literary critic and writer, her name is always associated with a long series of enormous, interesting interviews (1999-2005) with outstanding French-speaking authors, many of whom are famous worldwide: Michel Deguy, André Makine, Andrée Chedid, René de Obaldia, Eric-Emmanuel Schmitt, Vénus Khoury-Ghata, Olivier Roy, Tahar Ben Jelloun, Paule Constant, Bruno Etienne, Bruno Chenu, Jean Lacouture and others.

On the occasion of the francophone summit which took place in Lebanon in 2002, she published *Dialogue of Cultures and Love of the Language*. This book collected 22 of the above-mentioned literary dialogues.

As a translator she translated from French into Arabic the 450-page historical novel about Beirut, entitled *The Novel of Beirut* by Alexandre Najjar, as well as the novel *l'Imposture des mots* by Yasmina Khadra.

Studies

- Diploma of Higher Studies in Journalism and Communication from the University of Lebanon and Paris 2.

Among other distinctions

- The International Award for Excellence in Journalism of the International Catholic Union of the Press in 2001.

- The Prize of the Lebanese Ministry of Culture in 2000.

About Hanane Aad's Poetry

The latest poetry collection by the Lebanese poet Hanane Aad, entitled *I Carry My Freedom In My Mouth*, is distinguished by the quality of its language and by a recurrent rhetorical structure, although the latter never obscures or dilutes the poetical tension and power. What distinguishes it further are those poetical qualities that remind us of our literary ancestors, without overshadowing the author's specific fineness of emotion and excellence of style. There are features and accents reminiscent of the Biblical prophets, creating a spiritual and sacral tone and a meditative atmosphere, and in particular recalling Khalil Gibran's *The Prophet*.

- **Georges Geha,** Reuter's, 25 August 2010

Hanane Aad's poems reveal a quiet melancholy; her poetry is a whisper rather than an assertion. She knows how to rise above everyday language, yet uses it like her mother tongue, as the language of poetry. Hers is a finely chiselled writing, and her phrases are sculpted deeply.

- **Vénus Khoury-Ghata**, Paris 2000

Hanane Aad's *Pearls of the Soul Riding Virtue* displays a mystical awareness of the world, an intense language which combines intellect with intuition and also pays attention to the kind of poetical values which are absent from many works of poetry today.

   - Ahed Fadel, Al Hayat newspaper, 26 November 2006

Hanane Aad comes from a culture that is aware of the present epoch and of the value of its words. She writes a poetry equivalent to the pulse of the soul, to the importance of the virtue that she never ceases to search for and record, sometimes through the music of words, sometimes by a philosophy that we rarely find in the work of her fellow writers today.

   - Emily Nasrallah, Al Anwar newspaper, 2006

It is as if Hanane Aad, the poet who knows the secret of wisdom, were reassuring Al Hallaj when he was divided between two hearts: his heavenly one and his earthly one. The two main subjects of her verse, love and poetry, are expressed with eloquence and a beauty of language, and she displays great sincerity when writing about matters of the heart and the mind.

   - Dr. Sami Makarem, 27 April 2006

A language inlaid with metaphors and with existential and creative amazement. Did not Hanane Aad herself say that her language is at one and the same time her horse, her insight and her chivalry, or fouroussyah?

    - Dr. Amine Albert Al Rihani, 27 April 2006

The poetry of Hanane Aad is a laboratory of the soul's power and the will, and combines both the concrete and the abstract. Her poems are based on several contrasting themes, and the poetical element in them is a result of these contrasts being developed in a vertical sequence.

    - Salman Zayneddin, Al Anwar newspaper, 2006

Her poetry embodies a feeling of nihilism or absurdity, but in a positive sense, stimulating creation and innovation instead of death and surrender. This is the fruit of a transparent and sincere monologue, indicating the power of the heart and the power of the soul. The meditative inclination in Hanane Aad's verse may be founded on a strategy of her poetical writing to bring the abstract down from its throne to the level of the concrete and non absolute, in order to humanize what is abstract and to set up a possible dialogue with life, or the passing age, at least within the poem.

    - Jihad Hudeib, Amman, October 2004